GW01388454

YOUNG LEARNER'S
FIRST
DICTIONARY

Designed
and
illustrated by
Rachael O'Neill

zigzag

A dictionary is a book of words. It tells you what words mean and helps you check how to spell them.

This book explains more than 500 words. Each word, called a **headword**, is printed in heavy black type so that it is easy to find. The headword is followed by a **definition**, printed in ordinary type, which explains the meaning of the word. Some words are illustrated with pictures, to make the meanings clearer.

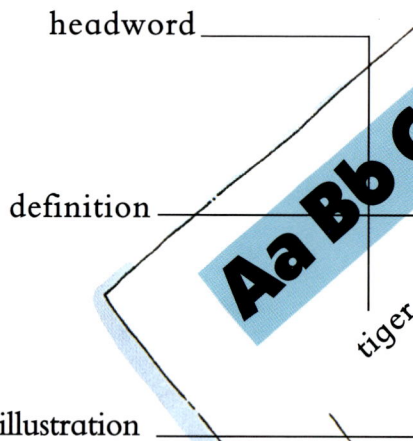

headword

definition

tiger

illustration

Aa Bb Cc Dd Ee Ff Gg Hh Ii I

A **tiger** is a wild animal with black and orange stripes. **Tigers** are big cats.

To look up a word – for example **tiger** – first look at the letter it begins with. Look at the letters at the top of these pages to find where "**t**" comes in the alphabet. You can see that it is near the end.

This tells you that the pages listing words beginning with "**t**" are near the end of the book. To help you, the letters "**Tt**" in the alphabet at the top of these pages are a different colour. To find the word **tiger,** look at its second letter and look at words beginning with "**ti**" If you cannot find it quickly, look at the third letter and try again.

The set of 26 letters across the top of the pages is called the alphabet. These are the signs we use to make the thousands of words in the English language.

The word "alphabet" comes from the first two letters of the ancient Greek alphabet, "alpha" and "beta".

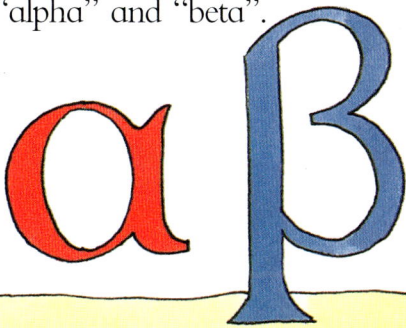

Look at the alphabets on the right. They are a few of the different alphabets used around the world today. Some of these letters look very different from the letters in our English alphabet.

АБГДЁЗ
Greek

بِسۡمِ ٱللَّهِ ٱلرَّحۡمَٰنِ
Arabic

ΕΖΗΘΙΚΛ
Russian

INTERNET LINKS

http://www.askoxford.com
Learn a new word every day, play lots of word games and discover some great facts about our language. There are also some tips for sending creative e-mails and text messages.

http://www.funbrain.com/detect/index.html
Create your own word search puzzles.

http://www.billsgames.com/wordscram
All sorts of word games – some are rather tricky!

http://www.littleexplorers.com/Dictionary.html
This easy-to-use picture dictionary is filled with links to child-friendly websites, along with activities and printouts to colour.

http://encarta.msn.com/quiz
Take the Encarta spelling test and see how you do! Scroll down to 'How Well Can You Spell?' This is a US site so some of the spellings may be a little different from British spellings.

http://www.foot-print.demon.co.uk/bslsite/b.html
Learn the British Sign Language alphabet with the help of animations.

http://www.surfnetkids.com/vocabulary.htm
A great directory for kids only! Check out the vocabulary page for links to daily activities to improve your spelling skills.

http://school.discovery.com/dictionaryplus
Along with the dictionary and thesaurus on this site, you'll find a crossword and anagram solver for those difficult puzzle clues!

http://www.netlingo.com
All the latest words in cyberspeak are explained here so you can be sure to keep up with the latest technology.

http://www.bbc.co.uk/education/revisewise/english/index.shtml
Choose from various activities designed to help your writing, spelling and much more. You can even submit your work to be shown on the site!

Aa

ache
An **ache** is a kind of pain. David's legs **ache** because he ran so fast.

address
Your **address** is the place where you live. When you send a letter you must write the **address** on it.

air
Air is all around us. We must breathe **air** to stay alive.

aircraft
An **aircraft** is a big flying machine such as an aeroplane.

alligator

An **alligator** has a long tail and a big mouth full of sharp teeth. **Alligators** live in rivers and swamps.

alphabet
The **alphabet** is the letters people use to write words.

angry
An **angry** person feels very cross and unhappy.

animal
An **animal** is a living thing that is not a plant. People, dogs, birds, frogs, spiders and fish are all **animals**.

answer
An **answer** is what people want when they ask a question. Jennifer **answered** her dad when he asked her a question.

ant
An **ant** is a tiny insect.

apple
An **apple** is a round fruit that grows on trees.

arm
Your **arm** is the part of your body that is between your shoulder and your hand.

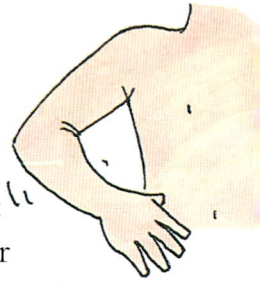

ask
You **ask** a question when you want to know something. You also **ask** when you want to have something.

asleep

When you are **asleep** your body is resting. Sue was so tired, she fell **asleep**.

aunt
Your **aunt** is your father's or your mother's sister. Your uncle's wife is your **aunt**, too.

awake
When you are **awake** you are not asleep. Sarah was still **awake** at ten o'clock.

Bb

baby
A **baby** is a very young child.

back
1. Your **back** is the part of your body behind you from your shoulders to your waist.
2. Kyle sat at the **back** of the class.

bad

1. A **bad** person does things that are wrong.
2. A **bad** cold can make you feel ill.

bag
You hold or carry things in a **bag**. Emily had some apples in a paper **bag**.

ball
A **ball** is a round toy. It is used in many games.

balloon
A **balloon** is a small rubber bag you blow into to fill it up with air.

banana
A **banana** is a fruit that grows on trees.

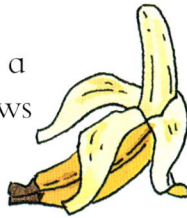

bark
1. **Bark** is the rough covering of a tree.
2. A **bark** is the loud sound a dog makes.

bat
1. A **bat** is a small flying animal. It has a furry body and wings made of stretchy skin.

2. You use a baseball **bat** to hit the ball in a game.

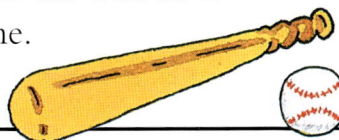

bear

A **bear** is a big furry wild animal. **Bears** can be fierce.

bed
A **bed** is something you sleep on. It is time to go to **bed**.

bee
A **bee** is a small flying insect.

bend
When you **bend** something you make it crooked.

best
When something is the **best** you like it the most. Jean is Betty's **best** friend.

better
1. Chris plays football **better** than he plays rugby.
2. If you are ill, medicine makes you **better**.

bicycle

A **bicycle** is something you ride on. **Bicycles** have two wheels.

big

Big means large. Our car is so **big** you can fit six people inside.

bird

A **bird** has feathers and wings. Most **birds** can fly.

birthday

Your **birthday** is the day of the year you were born. It is Jason's **birthday** on 16 January.

bite

To **bite** something means to cut it with your teeth. Charlene will **bite** into her apple.

blow

To **blow** means to move with air. The wind **blows** the leaves.

body

The **body** of a person or animal is every part of them.

bone

A **bone** is a hard part inside your body. You can feel the **bones** in your fingers.

book

A **book** is a number of printed pages joined together on one side. I am reading a **book**.

boot

You wear waterproof **boots** in the rain and snow.

born

When you are **born**, you begin living outside your mother. Nicole's baby sister was **born** last week.

bottle

A **bottle** is something you keep drinks in, such as milk, water or juice.

bottom

1. The **bottom** of something is its lowest part.

2. Your **bottom** is the part of your body on which you sit.

bounce

When a ball **bounces** it hits the ground and then goes up.

box

A **box** is made to hold things. John's toy car came in a red **box**.

bread

Bread is a food made from flour and milk. It is baked in the oven.

break

If something breaks it falls to pieces or stops working.

breath

Your breath is the air that goes in and out of your body all the time. Alan can hold his breath.

breathe

When you breathe, air goes in and out of your nose or your mouth.

bring

When you bring something you carry it with you. Bring a coat, it might get cold.

brother

Your brother is a boy who has the same parents as you.

brush

You use a brush for cleaning. Tony brushes his teeth carefully twice every day.

bug

A bug is an insect, like an ant or a bee.

build

When you build, you put something together. Katie is building a lovely castle from sand.

building

A building is a place where people live, work or play. Houses, hospitals and schools are buildings.

burn

If something burns, it is on fire. You put wood on the fire to help it burn.

bus

A bus is like a big car that carries a lot of people.

busy

When you are busy you have things to do. Julie is busy writing a letter.

butterfly

A butterfly is an insect with four large coloured wings.

buy

When you buy something you give money for it.

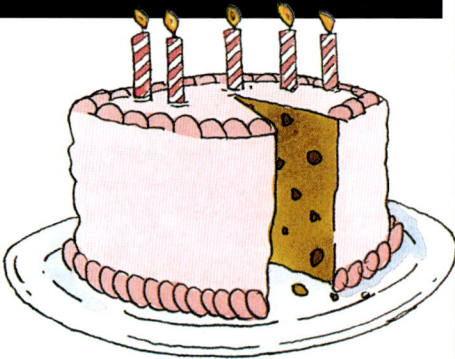

cake

A **cake** is made of flour, eggs and sugar. Rebecca had a **cake** on her birthday.

camel

A **camel** is a big animal that lives in hot deserts. **Camels** can live for days without food or water.

camera

You use a **camera** to take photographs or make movies.

can

A **can** is a metal container. It often holds food.

car

A **car** is a machine for people to ride in. The road was full of **cars**.

card

A **card** is made of stiff paper. **Cards** often have words and pictures on them. Jessica sent me a birthday **card**.

carry

When you **carry** something, you lift it and take it with you. Dad will **carry** a chair into the garden.

cat

A **cat** is a small animal with a long tail. **Cats** have soft fur.

catch

If you **catch** something you grab it or get it while it is moving. Michael threw the ball into the air and Ben tried to **catch** it.

chair

A **chair** is a piece of furniture for one person to sit down on.

change

If you **change** something you make it different. Kevin will **change** his dirty clothes for clean ones.

chase

When you **chase** something you go after it to try to catch it. The man **chased** the letter along the road.

cheese

Cheese is a food made from milk.

chest

1. Your **chest** is the part of your body at the front of you, from your neck to your waist.
2. A **chest** is a heavy box.

child

A **child** is a young boy or girl.

chin

Your **chin** is part of your face under your mouth.

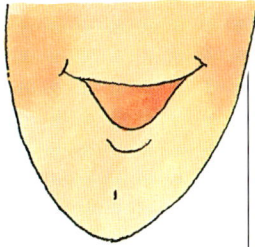

choose

When you **choose** you pick out something you want. Megan had to **choose** which sweet she wanted.

circle

A **circle** is round like a ring.

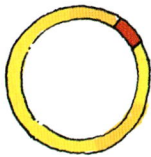

city

A **city** is a very busy place full of buildings. People live and work in **cities**.

class

A **class** is a group of people learning things together. The **class** is learning English.

clean

When you **clean** something you take the dirt off it. Joe must **clean** his muddy shoes.

clear

If something is **clear**, you are able to see through it. Windows are made of **clear** glass.

climb

When you **climb** you go up something high. Our cat **climbed** up a tree.

clock

A **clock** shows you the time.

close

1. When you **close** a door, you make it shut.
2. If you are **close** to a person or a thing, you are near them.

clothes

Clothes are the things that people wear to keep themselves warm. Shirts and socks are clothes.

cloud

Clouds float in the sky. They are made of tiny drops of water.

coat

When it is cold outdoors, a **coat** is something you put on over your other clothes to keep warm.

cold

1. A **cold** is something that makes you sneeze and feel ill.
2. If you are **cold** you should put on warmer clothes.

colour

1. Red, yellow, pink, green, purple and blue are different **colours**.
2. When you **colour** a picture you put red, blue or some other **colours** on it.

computer

A **computer** is a machine that can remember what you put into it. It can also find answers to questions.

copy

When you **copy** a thing you try to make something just like it. Robert **copied** his sister's drawing.

corner

A **corner** is where two things meet. In a room, the **corner** is where two walls come together.

cough

When you **cough** you make a sudden noise when air is pushed out of your throat. Michael has a bad **cough**.

count

You **count** to find out how many things there are.

country

1. A **country** is an area of land with its own people and language.
2. The **country** is land away from towns with farms and fields.

cousin

The children of your uncle or aunt are your **cousins**.

cover

When you **cover** something you put something over it.

cow

A **cow** is a large animal that lives on a farm. People drink the milk that comes from **cows**.

crash

1. A **crash** is a loud noise.
2. If something **crashes**, it falls or breaks into pieces.

crawl

When you **crawl** you move on your hands and knees.

cry

A **cry** is a noise you make when you are surprised or hurt. A baby **cries** when it needs milk.

cup

A **cup** is something that holds a drink. Joyce poured hot chocolate into a **cup**.

cut

1. When you **cut** something you change its shape with something sharp like scissors.
2. A **cut** is a small place on your skin that you hurt on something sharp.

dance

When you **dance** you move your whole body. People **dance** to music.

dangerous

If something is **dangerous** it might hurt you. A shark is a **dangerous** animal.

dark

When it is **dark** there is not enough light to see. If someone has **dark** hair it is usually brown or black.

daughter

If parents have a child who is a girl, she is their **daughter**.

day

1. **Day** is when it is light outside.
2. A **day** is 24 hours.

desert

A **desert** is a hot, dry area of land where very little rain falls.

dessert

Dessert is something sweet that you eat after a meal. Ice cream is a **dessert**.

different

When something is **different** it is not like anything else. That's not Nick's pen. It looks quite **different**.

dig

When people or animals **dig** they make a hole in the ground.

dinosaur

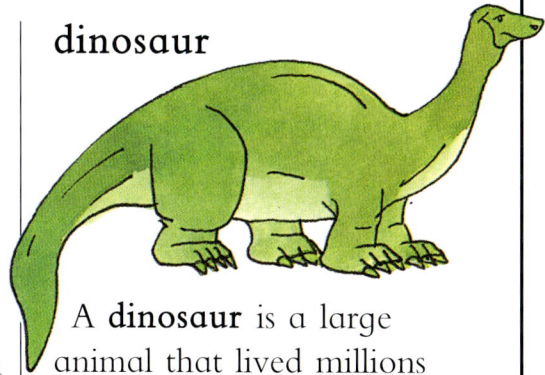

A **dinosaur** is a large animal that lived millions of years ago.

dirt

1. When something has **dirt** on it, it is not clean.
2. **Dirt** is the earth in which plants grow.

disappear

If something **disappears** you cannot see it any more. The magician made the rabbit **disappear**.

dog

A **dog** is a furry animal that barks.

door

A **door** opens to let you into a room.

draw

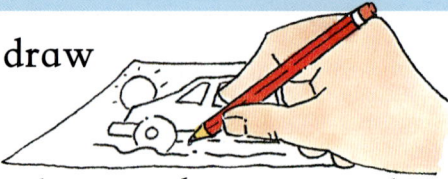

When you **draw**, you make a picture of something. Max likes to **draw** cars.

dress

1. You can **dress** yourself when you can put on your clothes without help.
2. A **dress** is a piece of clothing girls and women wear.

drink

When you **drink**, you swallow a liquid such as water. Milk and orange juice are **drinks**.

drop

1. If you **drop** something, you let it fall.
2. A **drop** is a tiny bit of liquid.

dry

If something is **dry**, it has no water in it. Christopher hung up the wet clothes to **dry**.

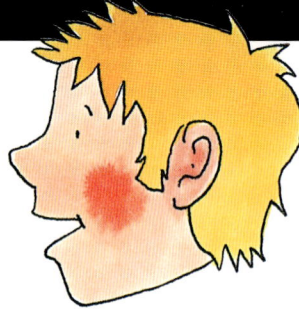

Ee

ear

You have two **ears** on your head. You use your **ears** to hear with.

earth

1. The **Earth** is the world we all live on.

2. The dirt that plants grow in is called **earth**.

easy

If something is **easy**, it is not difficult.

eat

When you **eat**, food goes in your mouth and down your throat to your stomach.

edge

The **edge** is the end or side of something flat. John's toy car fell off the **edge** of the table.

egg

Baby birds, fish and insects live inside **eggs** until they are ready to be born.

elbow

Your **elbow** is the part of your arm that bends.

elephant

An **elephant** is a very big animal. An **elephant** has a very long nose called a trunk.

empty

1. If something is **empty** there is nothing in it.
2. If you **empty** something, you take out everything in it. Adam **emptied** the bag.

end

The **end** of something is the last part. George is standing at the **end** of the line.

engine

An **engine** is something that makes a machine work. A car **engine** makes the car go.

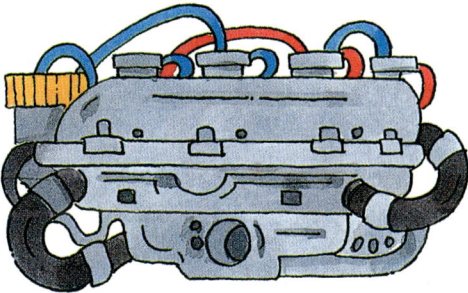

enjoy

If you **enjoy** something you like it very much. Jamie **enjoys** playing with his friends.

evening

Evening is the last part of day, before night. Do you watch television in the **evening**?

exciting

If you think something is **exciting** it is fun and you look forward to it. Travelling by train is very **exciting**.

expect

If you **expect** something to happen, you think it will happen. Carla **expects** to win the race.

explain

If you **explain** something to somebody you tell them about it so that they understand.

eye

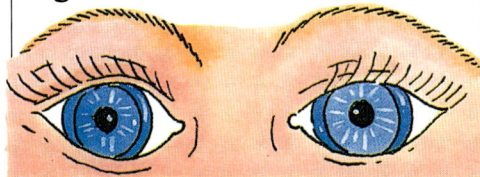

You have two **eyes** at the front of your head. You use your **eyes** to see things. What colour are your **eyes**?

Ff

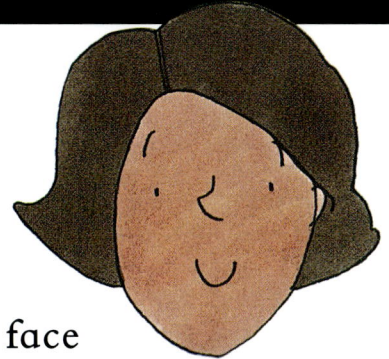

face

Your **face** is the front part of your head. Your eyes, nose and mouth are on your **face**.

fair

1. If something is **fair**, it is the right thing to do.
2. A **fair** is a place to go and have fun. People buy things at a **fair**.

fall

To **fall** means to drop to the ground.
The book **fell** off the shelf.

farm

A **farm** is a place where people keep animals or grow crops. Uncle Dan has cows on his **farm**.

fast

If someone or something is **fast** they can go very quickly. Nathan is a very **fast** swimmer.

father

A **father** is a man who has children.

favourite

Your **favourite** is the one you like better than all the others.
Ice cream is Justin's **favourite** dessert.

feather

Birds have **feathers** to keep them warm instead of fur or hair.

feed

When you **feed** a person or animal you give them something to eat. The mother bird **feeds** her babies.

feel

1. When you **feel** something, you touch it.
2. If you skip lunch you will **feel** very hungry.

field

A **field** is an open piece of land. Crops are grown in **fields**.

fierce

When an animal is **fierce** it is dangerous. Tigers can be very **fierce**.

fight

A **fight** is when people try to hurt each other. People usually **fight** because they are angry.

fill

If you **fill** something you put in as much as it will hold. Mum **filled** a bag with apples.

film

Film is something you put in a camera to take photographs.

find

When you **find** something you see what you are looking for. Brian **found** his shoes under the bed.

finger

Your **fingers** are part of your hands. People have five **fingers** on each hand.

finish

When you **finish** something you come to the end of it. Jennifer **finished** telling her story.

fire

Fire is what happens when something burns. The fire is hot!

first

When something is first, nothing else comes in front of it. Neil Armstrong was the first person to walk on the moon.

fish

A fish is an animal that swims and breathes in water. Fish live in seas and rivers.

fit

If something fits you it is the right size. Sarah's dress is too big. It does not fit.

fix

If somebody fixes something they make it work. Ask Dad to fix your bike.

flat

1. If something is flat, it is straight across.
2. When a balloon is flat, it has no air in it.

float

If something floats, it stays on top of water and does not go under it. The rubber duck is floating in the bath.

floor

The floor is the part of a room that you walk on.

flour

Flour comes from a plant called wheat. Bread and cakes are made from flour.

flower

A flower is part of a plant. Flowers often look colourful and smell sweet.

fly

1. To fly means to move through the air.
2. A fly is an insect with wings.

follow

If you follow someone you go along behind them. The children followed their mother into the store.

food

Food is what you eat. People and animals need food to live.

foot

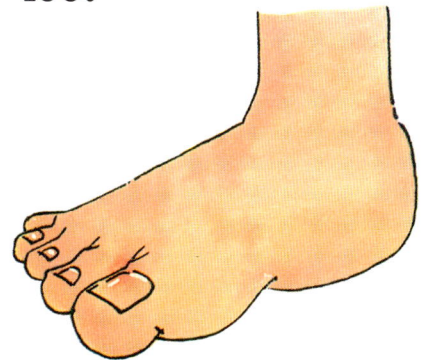

1. Your foot is at the end of your leg. You stand on your two feet.
2. A foot is also a unit of measure. There are 12 inches in one foot.

forget

If you **forget** something you do not think of it.

fresh

Fresh means new. Justin enjoys eating **fresh** biscuits.

friend

A **friend** is someone you like being with.

frightened

If you are **frightened** you are afraid. Tommy is **frightened** of spiders.

frog

A **frog** is a small animal that lives near ponds and rivers. **Frogs** have strong back legs that help them to jump a long way.

front

The **front** of something is usually the part that you see first. Alice has a house with a red **front** door.

frozen

Frozen food is made very cold so that it stays fresh for a long time.

fruit

Fruit is something to eat. Apples, lemons and bananas are different kinds of **fruit**.

full

If something is **full** there is no room left. Sarah's glass was **full** of chocolate milk.

fun

When you have **fun** you enjoy yourself. It is **fun** to play in the snow.

funny

Things that are **funny** make you laugh.

fur

Fur grows on the skin of animals. It keeps them warm.

Gg

game

A **game** is something you play. You can play **games** with your friends.

garage

A **garage** is a building. Cars are kept in **garages**.

garden

A **garden** is land where you can grow vegetables and flowers. Dad likes to dig in the **garden**.

give

When you **give** something to a person, you let them keep it. Jemma **gave** her friend a birthday present.

glass

1. **Glass** is used to make windows. You can see through **glass**.
2. A **glass** is something you drink from.

good

Something **good** makes you happy. This is a **good** book I'm reading.

grandfather

Your mother's father and your father's father are both your **grandfathers**.

grandmother

Your mother's mother and your father's mother are both your **grandmothers**.

grass

Grass is a green plant. Horses and sheep eat **grass**. **Grass** grows in many parks and gardens.

ground

The **ground** is the land you stand on when you are outside.

grow

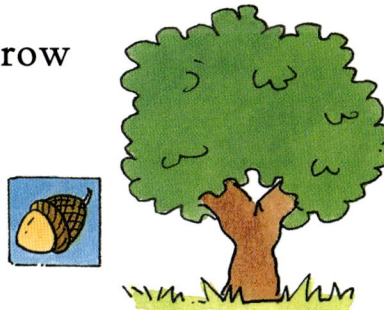

When things **grow** they get bigger. The oak tree had **grown** from an acorn.

guess

A **guess** is an answer you are not sure is right. **Guess** how old Deborah is?

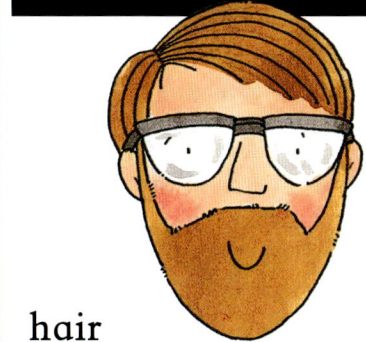

Hh

hair

Hair grows on people's heads. Dad's **hair** is brown.

hand

People have two **hands**. You use your **hands** to pick things up.

hang

When something **hangs** it is held up from the top. Alex **hung** up his coat.

happen

When things **happen**, they take place. What **happened** in school today?

happy

When you are **happy** you feel good about the way things are.

hard

1. If something is **hard** it does not change shape when you touch it.
2. Something that is **hard** to do can take a very long time. Fixing the bike was **hard**.

hate

If you **hate** doing something, you do not want to do it. Mark **hates** putting away his toys.

have

1. If you **have** something, you hold it or keep it.

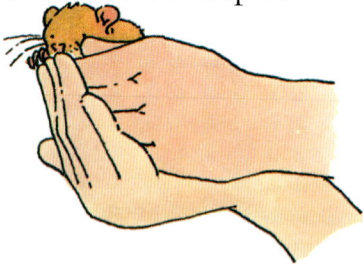

2. You can also **have** a good time at a party.

hear

You **hear** sounds with your ears. I can **hear** a dog barking.

heavy

If something is **heavy** it is hard to lift.

help

When you **help**, you do something for somebody. Do you need **help** carrying the bag?

hide

If you **hide** something, you put it where people cannot see it. Katherine **hid** the ball in the closet.

high

If something is **high**, it is a long way up. Emily's kite flew very **high** in the air.

hill

A **hill** is a high part of the land.

hit

If you **hit** something, you touch it quickly and hard. Jessica **hit** the ball a long way.

hold

If you **hold** something, you keep it in your hands or arms.

hole

1. A **hole** is a place that has been dug in the ground.
2. A **hole** is also a space in something. The mouse went into a **hole** in the wall.

home

Your **home** is the place where you live.

hope

If you **hope** for something, you want it to happen and think it will. Claire **hopes** to get a kitten soon.

horse

A **horse** is a big animal that you can ride. In the past, **horses** worked on farms.

hospital

A **hospital** is a place where sick people get better.

hot

Hot things burn if you touch them.

hour

An **hour** is a measure of time. There are sixty minutes in one **hour**, and twenty-four **hours** in one day.

house

A **house** is a building that people live in.

hungry

When you are **hungry** you want to eat.

hurricane

A **hurricane** is a very strong storm that can blow down trees and buildings.

hurry

When you **hurry** you move quickly.

hurt

When something **hurts**, it is painful. Josh **hurt** his knee when he fell.

husband

A **husband** is a man who is married.

Ii

ice

Ice is frozen water that feels cold and hard.

ice cream

Ice cream is a frozen food made of flavoured cream.

idea

When you have an **idea** you think of something to do.

important

Important things matter a lot. It is **important** to look and listen for traffic before you go across a road.

insect

An **insect** is a small animal with six legs. Ants, flies and bees are **insects**.

join

1. If you **join** two things, you put them together.
2. If you **join** a game, you become part of it.

joke

A **joke** is something to make you laugh. Dad put on a toy red nose as a **joke**.

juice

juice is the drink that comes from fruit like oranges.

jump

When you **jump** you bend your knees and push up in to the air. Cassie **jumped** high to catch the ball.

kangaroo

A **kangaroo** is a big animal with strong back legs. It moves along by jumping.

keep

1. If you **keep** something you have it. Pete asked if he could **keep** the book.
2. To **keep** quiet is to stay quiet.

kick

If you **kick** a ball you hit it with your foot. Dan gave the ball a hard **kick**.

kind

1. **Kind** means a group of things that are like each other. Bananas are a **kind** of fruit.
2. Someone who is **kind** thinks of other people and is good to them.

kiss

When you **kiss** someone you touch them with your lips. Mary gave William a **kiss**.

knee

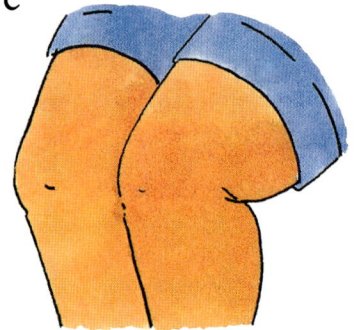

Your **knee** is the place where your leg bends. Ben fell and hurt his **knee**.

know

If you **know** something, you are sure about it.

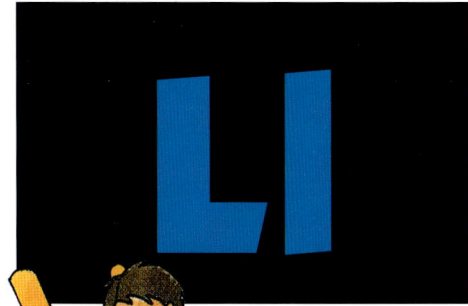

ladder

You use a **ladder** to climb up to and down from high places. Alan must use a **ladder** to get his cat down from the tree.

lamp

A **lamp** gives you light. James has a reading **lamp** by his bed.

land

1. **Land** is the dry part of the Earth.
2. When something **lands** it comes down from the air on to the ground.

last

When something is **last,** there is nothing else after it. Christopher ate the **last** piece of cake.

laugh

A **laugh** is the sound you make when you are happy. You **laugh** when you think something is funny.

leaf

A **leaf** is part of a plant. Most **leaves** are flat and green.

learn

When you **learn,** you find out something you did not know. Bonnie **learnt** to write last year.

left

You have a **left** side and a right side. In this picture, the boy is on the **left**.

leg

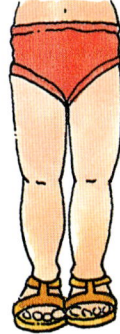

Your **legs** are part of your body. You use your legs for standing, walking and running.

lemon

A **lemon** is a yellow fruit that tastes sour.

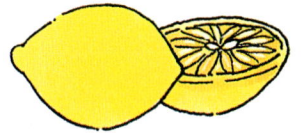

lesson

A **lesson** is something you learn. Tony's class had a writing **lesson** in school this morning.

letter

1. **Letters** make up words. A, B and C are **letters**.
2. A **letter** is a message you write on paper and send to another person.

lift
If you **lift** something, you pick it up. The bag was too heavy for Maggie to **lift**.

light
1. We need **light** to see by.
2. If something is **light** it is easy to lift.
3. If somebody **lights** a fire, they start it burning.

lightning
Lightning is a quick line of light in the sky. **Lightning** happens in a thunderstorm.

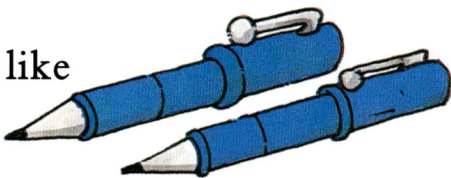

like
1. When one thing is **like** another thing, they are the same.
2. If you **like** a person, you feel happy with them.

line
1. A **line** is long and thin. Tamsin drew a straight **line**.
2. A **line** is a row of people.

lion
A **lion** is a wild animal. It is a big cat that lives in the jungle.

lip
Your **lips** are part of your mouth. You have two **lips**.

listen
When you **listen** to something you try and hear it as well as you can.

little
Little things are very small. The baby has **little** shoes.

live
1. To **live** is to be alive. Old people have **lived** for a long time.
2. When you **live** somewhere your home is there.

long
1. When something is **long,** the two ends are far apart.
2. **Long** is a measure of time. Is it a **long** time until your birthday?

look
You **look** at things with your eyes. **Look** at that bird.

loose
If something is **loose**, it is not tight. Mark's front tooth is **loose**.

lose
1. If you **lose** something, you don't know where it is.
2. If you **lose** a race you do not win.

loud
Something **loud** makes a lot of noise. Matt has a very **loud** voice.

love
Love is a very strong feeling for a person. If you **love** someone, you care about them very much.

low
Something **low** is not high up. Beatrice's television is on a **low** table.

machine

Machines help people to do things. A **machine** often has parts that move. You wash your clothes in a washing **machine.**

make

1. If you **make** something, you put it together.
2. You can **make** something happen. Richie **made** the baby laugh.

married

A man and woman who are **married** are husband and wife.

measure

If you **measure** something, you find out how big or heavy it is. Dad **measured** how tall Sonya had grown.

meat

Meat is part of an animal that people eat. Hamburgers are made of **meat.**

medicine

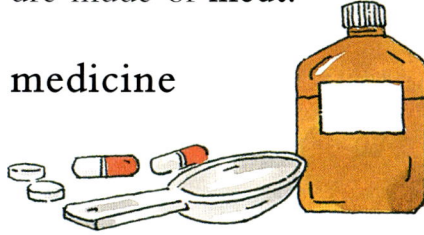

Medicine is something that helps sick people to get better. When Jon had a cough, his mother gave him **medicine.**

meet

If you **meet** someone, you get together with them. Mum **met** Marsha at school.

metal

Metal comes from the ground. Iron and silver are different kinds of **metal.** **Metal** is for making things like cars and machines.

middle

If you are in the **middle** of a row, you have the same number of people on each side of you.

milk

Milk is a drink. Most of the **milk** that people drink comes from cows.

minute

A **minute** is a measure of time. There are sixty seconds in a **minute.**

miss

1. If you **miss** something you do not get it.
2. If you **miss** someone, you are sorry they are not there.

mistake

If you make a **mistake** you get something wrong. I made a **mistake** in my spelling.

mix

When you **mix** things you put them together to make one thing.

money

You use **money** to buy things. **Money** can be coins or paper.

monkey

A **monkey** is a small animal that climbs trees. **Monkeys** have strong hands and tails.

month

A **month** is a measure of time. There are twelve **months** in a year.

moon

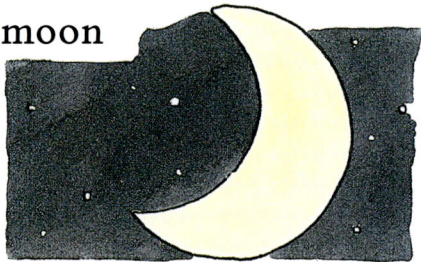

At night, you can often see the **moon** in the sky. It goes around the earth once every 28 days.

morning

Morning is the part of the day up to lunchtime.

mother

A **mother** is a woman who has children.

mountain

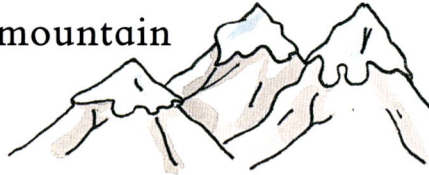

A **mountain** is a high piece of land that goes up into a point. **Mountains** are like very big hills.

mouse

A **mouse** is a small, furry animal. It has a pointed nose, sharp teeth and a long, thin tail.

mouth

Your **mouth** is part of your face. You open and close your **mouth** to speak and to eat.

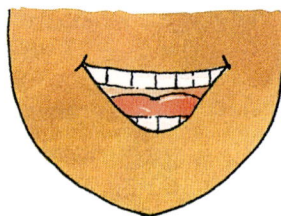

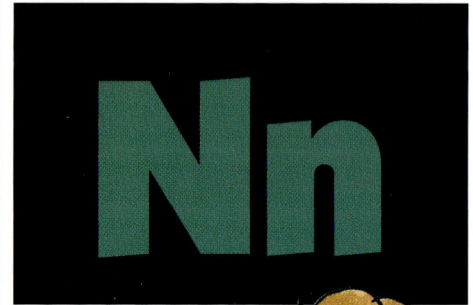

Nn

name

A **name** is what people or things are called. My friend's **name** is Julia.

neck

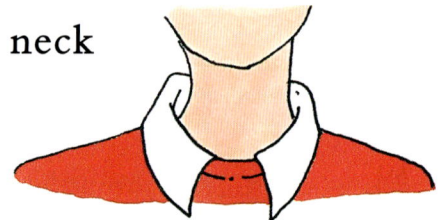

Your **neck** is the part of your body from your head to your shoulders.

need

If you **need** something you must have it. Kay **needs** to have new shoes.

nephew

The son of a person's sister or brother is their **nephew.**

new

New things have not been used. Cindy was given a new dress for the party.

niece

The daughter of a person's sister or brother is their niece.

night

Night is when the sky is dark.

noise

A noise is a kind of sound. The children shouted and made a lot of noise.

nose

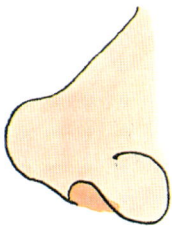

Your nose is part of your face. You smell things with your nose.

number

You use numbers when you count things or people. One hundred is a big number.

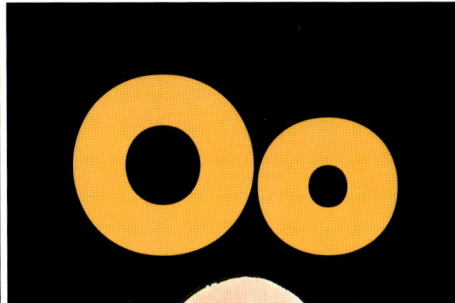

Oo

old

1. If someone is old they have lived for a long time.
2. You say something is old if you have used it a lot.

open

If something is open it is not covered or shut. Will you open the door for me, please?

orange

An orange is a round, juicy fruit that grows on trees.

outside

If you are outside, you are not in a building. When it is sunny, we like to go outside to play.

owl

An owl is a bird. Owls fly at night.

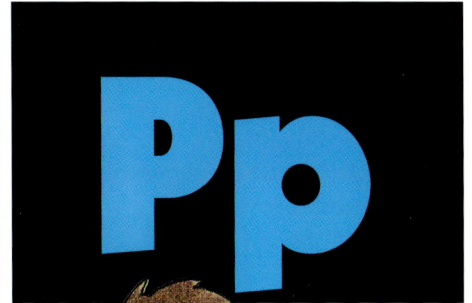

Pp

pain

A pain is what you feel when you are hurt or ill. When Lee fell off his bike he had a bad pain in his arm.

paint

When you paint something, you put colour on it. What colour paint shall we use for the door?

paper

You can write or draw on paper. Coloured paper can be used to wrap presents.

park

1. A **park** is a place with grass and trees. People rest or play games in a **park**.
2. If someone **parks** a car, they leave it somewhere for a while. Mum **parked** the car in the garage.

part

A **part** of something is a piece of it. Your arm is **part** of your body.

party

A **party** is a group of people having a good time. Vic will have a **party** on his birthday.

pencil

A **pencil** is a wooden stick with black or colour inside. You draw or write with a **pencil**.

photograph

A **photograph** is a picture you make with a camera. Mum **photographed** Daniel playing in the sand.

piano

A **piano** is a musical instrument. You play the **piano** with your fingers.

pick

1. When you **pick** things like flowers or fruit, you take them from the place where they grow.
2. If you **pick** things up, you lift them.
3. If there are things to choose from, you **pick** the one you want.

picture

A **picture** is something you draw. Marie drew a **picture** of her sister.

piece

A **piece** of something is a bit of it. Would you like a **piece** of cake?

pig

A **pig** is an animal that lives on a farm. We eat meat from **pigs**.

place

A **place** is where something happens or where something is. Let's find a good **place** for our party.

plain

1. A **plain** is a large, flat part of land.
2. If something is **plain**, it is all one colour.

plant

A **plant** is something living that grows in dirt. Many **plants** have leaves and colourful flowers.

plate

A **plate** is flat and round. You eat your food from a **plate**.

play

1. When you **play**, you do something that is fun.
2. If you **play** music, you make music.

playground

A **playground** is a place where children can play. Bill likes to play on the slide in the **playground**.

point

1. The **point** of something is the sharp end of it.
2. You **point** your finger to show someone the way, or to show them where something is.

pour

When you **pour** something, you tip it out. Roger **poured** some milk from the bottle.

present

A **present** is something that people give. Hector had lots of **presents** on his birthday.

promise

If you **promise** something, you are saying you are sure you will do it. Betsy **promises** to take the dog for a walk.

pull

When you **pull** something, you move it towards you.

push

When you **push** something, you move it away from you. Catherine **pushed** open the door with her hand.

put

If you **put** something in a place, you make it go there. Tom **put** the food on the plate.

Qq

question

You ask a **question** when you want to know something.

quick

When something is **quick**, it does not take a long time.

quiet

If you are **quiet**, you do not make any noise. The class was very **quiet**.

Rr

rabbit

A **rabbit** is a small, furry animal. **Rabbits** have long ears and short, fluffy tails.

race

When you run a **race**, you find out who goes the fastest. Sam will **race** you to the shops.

rain

Rain is water that falls in drops from the sky.

rainbow

A **rainbow** is a band of colours you can sometimes see in the sky. **Rainbows** happen when there is sun and rain together.

read

People who **read** can understand words written down.

ready

When you are **ready**, you can start to do something. Are you **ready** to go to school?

remember

When you **remember** something, you can think of it again. Do you **remember** when we sailed in the boat?

rest

When you **rest**, you stay quiet for a while. Grandma likes to have a **rest** every day.

rhyme

When words **rhyme**, they have the same sound. Cat and bat are words that **rhyme**.

ride

When you **ride** something, you sit on it as it moves along. Would you like a **ride** on my bike?

right

1. You have a left side and a **right** side. Many people write with their **right** hand.
2. If you are **right** about something, you know the answer.

ring

1. A **ring** is something you wear on your finger.
2. A **ring** is also the sound made by the telephone.

river

A **river** is a lot of water flowing across the land.

road

A **road** is a narrow, clear piece of land. People build **roads** for trucks and cars to drive on.

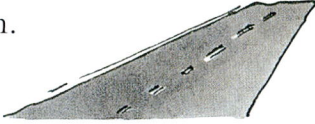

rock

Rocks are very hard, big stones in the earth.

roll

1. When something **rolls**, it turns over and over.
2. A **roll** is a small piece of bread.

room

1. A **room** is part of a house or other building.
2. **Room** also means space. Is there enough room?

row

If people or things are in a **row**, they are in a line. Natalie put her toy cars in a **row**.

run

When you **run**, you go as fast as you can on foot.

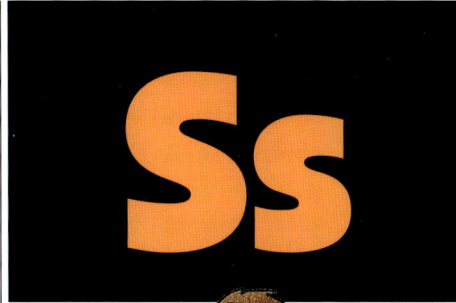

Ss

safe

When you are **safe**, nothing bad can happen to you.

salt

Salt is something people put on food to make it taste better.

same

1. Things that are the **same** are alike. Jan's hair is the **same** colour as her sister's hair.

sand

Sand is tiny pieces of rock. You find **sand** in deserts and on beaches.

say

When you **say** something, you speak. Jeffrey **says** he is going to the park.

scare

If something **scares** you, it makes you feel frightened.

school

School is a place where people go to learn things.

scissors

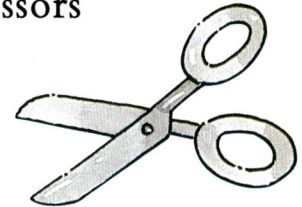

Scissors have two sharp parts joined in the middle. You use **scissors** for cutting.

sea

The **sea** is a very large area of saltwater.

second

1. **Second** is the next thing after first.
2. A **second** is a measure of time.

see

When you **see**, you use your eyes to look at something. Can you **see** those birds?

seed

A **seed** is the part of a plant that will make another plant.

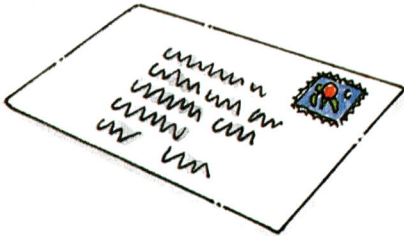

send

If you **send** something, you make it go somewhere else. Pat **sent** Grandpa a birthday card.

shape

A **shape** is the way something looks. The letter Z has a zigzag **shape**.

share

If you **share** something, you give a part of it to somebody else. Amanda and her sister **shared** an apple.

sharp

Something **sharp** is easy to cut with. You must be careful with **sharp** scissors.

sheep

A **sheep** is an animal that lives on a farm. **Sheep** are kept for wool and meat.

sheet

1. A **sheet** is a large piece of cloth you put on a bed.
2. A **sheet** of paper is a flat piece of paper.

shell

A **shell** is a hard cover. A snail has a **shell** on its back.

ship

A **ship** is a large boat that carries people and things.

shoe

Shoes are things you wear on your feet. You can walk outside in **shoes**.

shop

You **shop** when you want to buy something. Mum wants to **shop** for a new dress.

short

1. A **short** person is not very tall.
2. A **short** walk does not take a long time.

shoulder

Your **shoulder** is the place where your arm joins your neck.

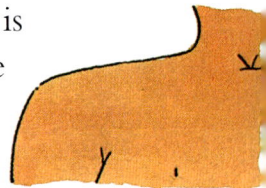

shout

You **shout** when you make a loud noise with your voice.

show

1. You **show** something when you let a person see it.
2. A **show** is something you see.

shut

If something is **shut**, it is not open. Please **shut** the window.

sick

If you are **sick**, there is something wrong with your body. Jo is too **sick** to go to school.

side

1. A **side** is a part of something.
2. In a game, people play on different **sides**.

sing

People who **sing** make music with their voices.

sister

Your **sister** is a girl who has the same parents as you.

sit

To **sit** means to rest on your bottom. The children **sat** on the floor.

size

Size is how big something is. These shoes are the wrong **size**!

skin

Skin is the thin outer cover of living things. An apple has a thin **skin**.

sky

The **sky** is all the space above you outside. The sun, moon and stars are in the **sky**.

sleep

You **sleep** when you close your eyes and rest your whole body. Sarah needs more **sleep**.

slide

1. When you **slide**, you move along easily on something slippery, like ice.
2. A **slide** is something you play on.

slip

If you **slip**, you slide too fast and fall down. Lynn **slipped** on the wet grass.

slow

Slow people or animals don't move very quickly. Snails are very **slow**.

small

Small things are quite little. Most insects are **small**.

smell

If food has a bad **smell**, usually it is not fresh. You **smell** things with your nose.

smile

When you **smile**, the ends of your mouth go up. The baby gave a **smile**.

smoke

Smoke is the dark cloud that comes from something burning.

snail

A snail is a very small animal with a shell on its back. Snails move by sliding slowly along the ground.

sneeze

When you sneeze, air blows out of your nose and mouth with a loud noise. Sam sneezes when he has a cold.

snow

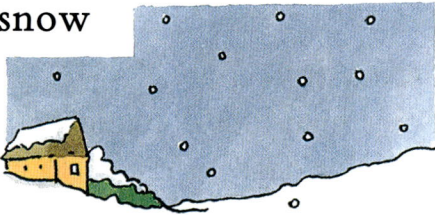

Snow is frozen water that falls from the sky. Snow is soft and white.

soap

People clean themselves with soap.

sock

Socks are soft clothes you wear on your feet.

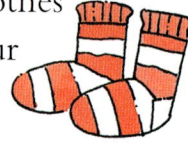

soft

1. If you touch something soft, it does not feel hard.
2. A soft noise is very quiet.

son

If parents have a child who is a boy, he is their son.

sorry

You are sorry when you feel bad about something. Lonnie is sorry she cannot come to the party.

sound

A sound is something you can hear. That sounds like a dog barking.

sour

Something that is sour has a sharp taste. Lemons are sour.

space

1. A space is like a hole or a place with nothing in it.
2. The Moon, Sun, and Earth are all in space.

speak

When you speak, you say words. Please speak quietly.

special

Something that is special is important and different from anything else. Mum made a special dress for the party.

speed

Speed is how fast something goes. What speed can your car go?

spell

When you spell a word, you put the letters in the right places. C-A-T spells cat.

spend

To spend money or time means to use it. Would you like to spend a day at the zoo?

spider

A **spider** is a small animal with eight legs. **Spiders** build webs and catch insects to eat.

square

A **square** is a shape that has four sides all the same. The rooms in Marta's house are all **square**.

stairs

Stairs are a set of steps inside a house or other building.

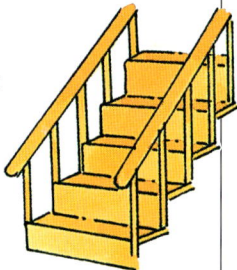

stand

When you **stand**, you are on your feet. Dad had to **stand** in line to get on the bus.

start

1. You **start** to do something when you begin it.
2. The **start** of a TV show or movie is the beginning.

state

A **state** is one part of a country. There are fifty **states** in the U.S.A.

stay

When you **stay** in a place, you don't leave it. Ed has to **stay** in his room to finish his homework.

step

1. You take a **step** when you pick up your foot and move it to a different place.
2. A **step** is also something you walk on to go up or down.

stick

1. A **stick** is a long, thin piece of wood.
2. You can **stick** a poster on the wall with tape.

stone

A **stone** is a small rock that comes out of the ground. Some buildings are made of big **stones**.

stop

If you **stop** doing something, you don't do it any more. Angie **stopped** reading her book.

store

A **store** is a place that sells things. Ken went to the **store** to buy some apples.

storm

When there is a **storm**, it rains or snows and it is very windy. Thunder and lightning sometimes happen in **storms**.

story

A **story** is about something that has happened. Some **stories** are made up, and some are about real things.

straight

Something that is **straight** does not bend. Can you draw a **straight** line?

strange

If something is **strange**, it is new to you.

street

A **street** is a road with buildings on it.

stretch

When something **stretches**, it becomes longer. I **stretched** to reach the top shelf.

strong

1. If something is **strong** it does not break easily.
2. **Strong** winds blow very hard.
3. Someone who is **strong** can lift heavy things easily.

sugar

Sugar is sweet and made from plants. People put **sugar** in foods and drinks to make them taste sweet.

sun

The **sun** is in the sky. It gives us heat and light.

sure

If you are **sure** something is true, you know you are right about it.

surprise

A **surprise** is something you do not know about before it happens. Mum and Dad **surprised** Teresa on her birthday.

sweet

Things that are **sweet** have lots of sugar in them. Cakes and ice cream are **sweet**.

swim

When you **swim**, you move your arms and legs to go along in the water.

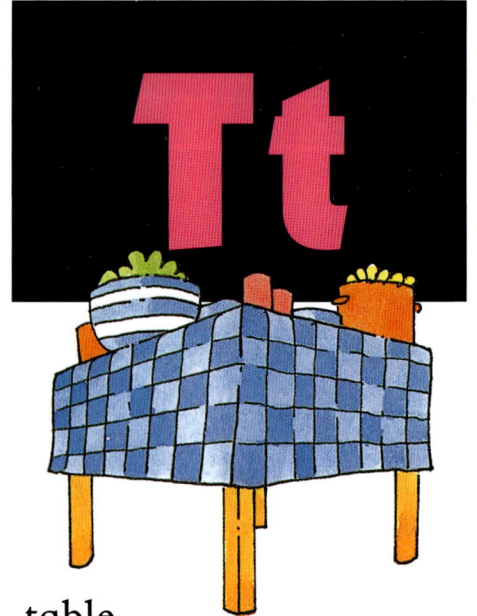

Tt

table

A **table** has legs and a flat top. Hurry now, the food is on the **table**.

tail

A **tail** grows at the back end of some animals. Dogs and cats have **tails**.

talk

When you **talk**, you speak words. Shaun's baby sister is learning to **talk**.

tall

Someone who is **tall** has grown higher than other people. Monica's dad is **taller** than her mum.

taste

When you **taste** something, you feel it with your mouth and tongue. Lemons **taste** sour.

teach

When somebody **teaches** you, they help you learn how to do something. Mum will **teach** Bernie to swim.

team

A **team** is a lot of people working or playing together. You need two **teams** to play baseball.

tear

You **tear** something when you pull it apart. James's dog likes to **tear** paper.

teeth

Your **teeth** are inside your mouth. You use your **teeth** for eating food.

telephone

A **telephone** lets you talk to someone who is somewhere else. Another word for **telephone** is **phone**.

television

You can see pictures and hear sounds on a **television**. **TV** is another name for **television**.

tell

If somebody **tells** you something, they let you know about it. **Tell** Mum what you did at school.

temperature

The **temperature** of something is how hot or cold it is.

think

When you **think** about something, you have it in your mind. Can you **think** about a present for Mum?

thirsty

If you are **thirsty**, you want something to drink.

throat

Your **throat** is the part of your body that is inside your neck. When you are thirsty, your **throat** feels dry.

throw

When you **throw** something, you send it through the air with your hand. Jesse **threw** the ball a long way.

thumb

Your **thumb** is the finger near your wrist. Your **thumb** helps you pick up things.

thunder

Thunder is the loud noise that you hear in a storm. **Thunder** follows lightning.

tie

1. You **tie** something when you fasten the ends together.
2. A **tie** is something men wear around their shirt collars.

tiger

A **tiger** is a wild animal with black and orange stripes. **Tigers** are big cats.

tight

1. If clothes are too **tight**, they are not big enough.
2. If you hold something **tight**, you won't drop it.

time

We measure **time** in seconds, minutes, hours, days, weeks, months and years. Look at the clock and see the **time**.

tiny

Things that are **tiny** are very, very small. Ants are **tiny** insects.

tired

If you feel **tired**, you want to rest or fall asleep.

toe

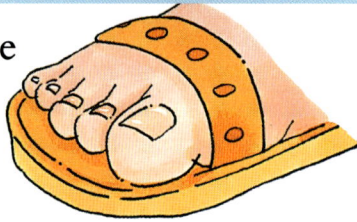

Your **toes** are part of your body. You have five **toes** at the end of each foot.

tongue

Your **tongue** is inside your mouth. Your **tongue** helps you to speak and to taste food.

top

1. A **top** is a toy that spins very fast.
2. The **top** of something is its highest part.

tornado

A **tornado** is a very strong wind that spins fast in the air.

touch

When you **touch**, you feel things with your hands. Ice is cold to **touch**.

town

A **town** is a place where people live and work. **Towns** are smaller than cities.

toy

A **toy** is something you play with. A doll and a ball are both **togs**.

traffic

Traffic is cars, bicycles and trucks travelling on the road. When there is a lot of **traffic**, the road is very busy.

train

Trains carry people and things quickly from one place to another. A **train** is pulled along by an engine.

tree

A **tree** is a very big plant with leaves and a trunk.

triangle

1. A **triangle** is a shape with three straight sides.
2. A **triangle** is something you can play music on.

truck

A **truck** is like a big, strong car that carries things. Trucks travel on the road.

true

When something is **true**, it is right. **True** stories are about things that really happen.

try

If you **try** to do something, you see if you can do it. Joan will **try** to lift the heavy chair.

turn

1. When you **turn**, you move around in a circle.
2. When it is your **turn**, it is time for you to do something. It was Robert's **turn** to play.

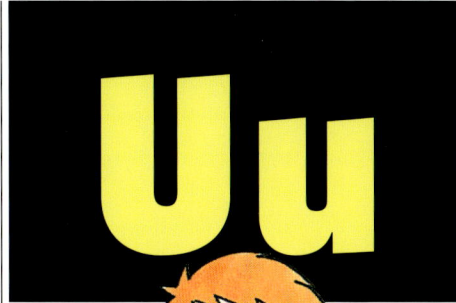

Uu

uncle

Your father's brother and your mother's brother are your **uncles**.

understand

You **understand** when you know what something means. A dictionary helps you **understand** new words.

use

When you **use** a thing, you do something with it. Tammy **uses** a spoon to stir the soup.

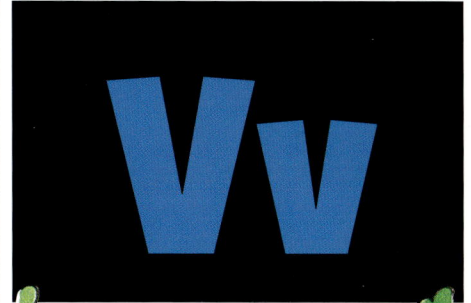

Vv

valley

A **valley** is the low land between hills.

vegetable

A **vegetable** is a plant that you can eat. Carrots and potatoes are **vegetables** that grow under the ground.

video

A **video** has sound and pictures on it. To watch a **video**, you put it in a machine hooked up to a television.

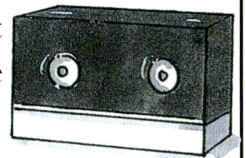

voice

Your **voice** is the sound you make when you speak or sing.

wait

When you **wait**, you stay where you are for a time. **Wait** here while I make a phone call.

waiter

A **waiter** is a person who brings you food in a restaurant.

walk

You **walk** by putting one foot in front of the other. Sometimes, Jamie **walks** to school.

wall

1. The **walls** of a room are the sides of it.
2. Some gardens have **walls** around them.

want

When somebody **wants** something, they hope to get it. Melissa **wants** a new doll for her birthday.

warm

Warm is between hot and cold. Adam washed his face with **warm** water.

wash

When you **wash** something you use soap and water to make it clean. Mandy helped Mum **wash** the car.

watch

1. If you **watch** a person or a thing, you look to see what is happening.

2. A **watch** is a small clock you wear on your wrist.

water

There is **water** in seas and rivers. Fish live in **water**.

wave

1. When you **wave** to someone, you move your hand in the air.
2. **Waves** are parts of the sea that move up and down.

way

1. The **way** somebody does something is how they do it.
2. The **way** to a place is how you get there.

weak

If people or things are **weak**, they are not very strong.

wear

1. When you **wear** something, you have it on your body.
2. When something **wears** out, it gets too old to use.

weather

The **weather** is how it is outside. It snows when the **weather** is cold.

week

A **week** is a measure of time. Seven days make one **week**.

weigh

You **weigh** something to find out how heavy it is. Dad **weighed** the sugar and flour when he made a cake.

wet

Something **wet** has water on it or in it.

wheel

A **wheel** is round. Cars and bicycles move on **wheels**.

whisper

When you **whisper**, you say something very quietly.

whole

Whole means every part of something. Karen ate the **whole** cake.

wife

A **wife** is a woman who is married.

wild

If something is **wild**, it is not tame or quiet. Most **wild** animals live far from towns and cities.

win

When you **win**, you do best of all. Kelly **won** the swimming race.

wind

Wind is moving air. The strong **wind** blew the leaves from the trees.

window

A **window** is a space in a wall that lets in air and light. **Windows** have glass in them to keep out wind and rain.

wing

Birds and some insects have **wings**. They use their **wings** for flying.

wish

When you **wish** for something, you want it to happen.

wood

Wood comes from trees. It is used to make furniture, like tables and chairs.

wool

Wool is the coat of a sheep. People make **wool** into clothes.

word

People use **words** when they speak or write. "Cat", "funny" and 'jump' are all **words**.

work

1. **Work** is a job that a person does for money. Dad **works** in a store.
2. If something **works**, it is not broken. Mum fixed the TV and now it **works**.

world

The **world** is the Earth that we all live on.

worry

When you **worry**, you think things will go wrong. David **worries** that he will be late for school.

write

When you **write**, you use a pen or pencil to make words on paper.

wrong

If something is **wrong**, it is not right. The answer to the question was **wrong**.

x-ray

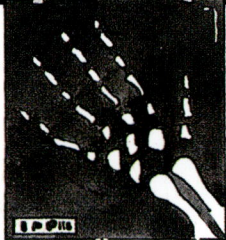

An **x-ray** is a picture of the inside of a person's body.

yacht

A **yacht** is a kind of large boat. People race **yachts**, or ride in them for fun.

yard

1. A **yard** is a measure to tell you how long something is. One **yard** is three feet.
2. A **yard** is also the land around a house.

year

A **year** is a measure of time. There are twelve months in a **year**.

young

If someone is **young**, they were born a short time ago. A kitten is a **young** cat.

zebra

A **zebra** is a wild animal. **Zebras** look like horses with black and white stripes on their bodies.

zigzag

A **zigzag** is a line that bends one way and then the other.

zoo

A **zoo** is a place where wild animals are kept. People can see the animals in a **zoo**.

First published in 1994

This edition published in 2002 by Zigzag Children's Books, a division of Chrysalis Books plc
64 Brewery Rd, London N7 9NT

Copyright © Zigzag Children's Books
Printed and bound in China

ISBN   1 903 954 169 (hardback)
       1 903 954 193 (paperback)